The publisher has strived to be as accurate and complete ⌄ possible in the creation of this
book. The book is not intended for use as a source of medical, or healing advice. All readers are
advised to services of competent professionals in coaching, medical and therapeutic fields.

In a practical advice book, as with anything in life, there are no guarantees of progress made.
Readers are cautioned to rely on their own judgement about their individual circumstances and
to act accordingly.

While all attempts have been made to verify the information provided for this publication, the
publisher assumes no responsibility for errors, omissions, or contrary interpretation of the
subject matter herein. Any perceived slights of specific persons, peoples, or organisations are
unintended

Don't event THINK about mobility training, improving movement or trying to prevent injury...

WAIT UNTIL YOU'VE READ THIS GUIDE!

I can promise you...

You're going to have a DIFFERENT APPROACH!

If you are doing (or even getting ready to do) any one of these things, with your clients **STOP!**

 Foam Rolling

 Stretching

 Strength Training

 Warming Up

 Cooling Down

 Programming Sessions

 Delivering Sessions

 Doing course after course to keep learning

There's nothing wrong with these techniques, in fact, some of them are vital to the safety of your sessions, but we're going to take them (and your coaching skills) to the next level!

Are you ready?

Welcome to the Guide
Here's How to Succeed with This Guide

The Coronavirus of 2020 changed EVERYTHING for sports and fitness coaches. It showed us just how vulnerable our clients are when the healthcare and other medical support networks are shut down and unable to help with their injuries

It showed us how reliant we've become on the **treatment** of injuries and the HUGE opportunities available to us as coaches to not only help prevent these problems, but to stand head and shoulders above all the other coaches out there as we do it.

Trust me when I say...

IT'S IN YOUR BEST INTEREST TO READ EVERY WORD OF THIS GUIDE, *UNDERSTAND IT*, AND IMPLEMENT IT!

There's over 30 years of fitness coaching, movement analysis, injury prevention and injury treatment speaking here. I'll tell you more about myself in a minute but first **let's get back to you**!

Your income relies on attendance to your sessions and the results you can generate from them, so it's paramount that you keep your clients training consistently.

But the chances are that you aren't **spending much time on mobility** in your sessions right now.

I've taught **countless coaches and individuals** how to blend my unique injury prevention methods into their training sessions so that they don't have to spend extra time on mobility or try to convince clients to do it - they can simply get on with what they love!

I've created the simplest processes, systems and approach that will do **95% of the work for you** - and I can guarantee that it's unlike anything you've ever seen before!

You will be able to build this strategy on your own, but there are also groups, trainings and services that can assist you as well.

Who is This Guide For?

Make sure this guide is for YOU before you read any further!

This guide was written specifically for:

Parent volunteer coaches, club coaches, part-time group instructors, Physical Education teachers, and full-time fitness professionals of all kinds!

In other words:

- Coaches who care about the welfare of their clients (even after the session has ended)
- Coaches who love to watch their clients succeed
- Coaches who love to make a difference

These methods are **NOT** created for assistant coaches or newly qualified coaches - there's far too much already on your plate, thinking about how to coach without overwhelming you with even *more* techniques!

To make sure that you have the right foundation to succeed with injury prevention, you'll need to have a **valid certification that qualifies you to run your own sessions without supervision.**

That means that your Governing Body recognizes you as a qualified coach within their organization and you are confident running your own sessions. You may not have any mobility or injury prevention experience yet, but that's okay.

We just need to **make sure the foundation is in place!**

The Choice is Yours
I don't think you have a choice!

I'm from Yorkshire in the UK and Yorkshire folk have a reputation for straight talking. That's why I'm going to be straight with you. My guess is that you are reading this guide because you trying to figure out how you can **do more to help your clients avoid injury.**

I don't know why you decided to do this right now, but obviously you don't have the answer you were looking for, otherwise you wouldn't need to **explore what I have to say.**

The truth is, most people won't read every word in this guide. They won't take action and that won't benefit the clients they say they're trying to help. <u>There are many reasons for that</u>. Some think it's too hard or they don't believe they can. Some think they know it all, so they won't even try. Some don't consider it important enough, but the most common reason (by a long way!) is that they think that it won't work for them.

If you're one of those people, then you have my permission to stop reading this guide right now. Why? **Because you've already set yourself up to fail**! Can you see how you are what you think?

Is it easy to prevent injuries? No. But it's not as difficult as the industry makes out either. In fact, I'm doing everything I can to help simplify the process for you. I'm going to introduce you to the **VERY BEST** mobility strategies in the industry.

Every strategy I'm about to reveal has been **100% created by me**. There is nothing I stole from anybody else, and where others have inspired me, I will absolutely give credit where credit is due.

I ask that you make a commitment RIGHT NOW! Be open-minded, positive and have the discipline and consistency to make it through this guide. If you don't understand everything you read right now, that's okay.

I am here to help you and have a community you can join when you're done reading this. I also have coaching programs and workshops, so rest assured **you're in GREAT HANDS!**

Let's GO!

Here's What We're Going to Cover...

Who Am I?

My name is Sarah J Pitts

I've been coaching fitness since I was 13 years old, when I would assist my PE teachers with
lunchtime & extra-curricular sports for the kids who were younger than me.
You'll learn about my expertise as you go through this guide.

However, I want you to know that I have also been assessing movement, treating and preventing injuries for over a decade.

I've been on a mission for the last 5 years to create a simple solution for those coaches who want to do more to help their clients avoid injury without overstepping their role as a coach or being drawn into becoming a therapist.

Here are some facts about me:

- Been in the industry since 1991
- Worked as a Fitness Instructor, Personal Trainer, Corrective Exercise Specialist and Soft-Tissue Therapist
- Creator of the SMARTT® methods. The injury prevention approach that is changing the face of fitness.
- Helped countless individuals out of pain who had given up hope of ever finding a long-term solution
- Taught coaches across the world who are, in turn helping people out of pain and preventing countless more from developing pain in the first place
- Provide REAL solutions to the seemingly inevitable injury problem
- Massive dog lover and proud owner of Belle, my "rescue ratbag"

What Would it Be Like...
Stop and think for a moment

What would it be like if you had a community that was consistent and reliable in their attendance? Or if they were **excited and looking forward to coming to your sessions?**

How amazing would it feel if you could **create endless variety in your sessions**, so you'd <u>never run out of ideas</u> and look like the ROCKSTAR coach you were destined to be?

What if you were able to assess for and identify potential problems simply by watching your clients train? Your clients would think you had **superpowers** and be lining up to join your sessions!

What if you didn't have to change anything about how you coach, and you could use your existing skills to start making a REAL difference? How about if you had a **catalogue of ready-made videos** available for your clients to follow that allowed you to <u>charge much more than other coaches</u>?

What if you had step-by-step instructions that showed you EXACTLY how to have everything I listed above? What if you were part of a community of people who were all trying to achieve the same thing? What if there were **training programs, certifications and tools that would help you hit the ground running**? What if...?

What if *this is your solution*?

When it Comes to Actually **Preventing** Sporting Injuries...

This is the BEST SOLUTION!

The Principles of Injury Prevention
2 minutes and 9 seconds that will show you the way

You may be the most experienced coach in the world, so you may be saying...come on Sarah, just show me how to prevent injuries! My response to you is that I'm doing just that, right this minute.

YOU HAVE TO WATCH THIS VIDEO! https://bit.ly/cesar-lessons-video

Here's the reason why. I'm going to do everything I can to show you the way. **You're going to have the entire blueprint**

You're going to know the **systems, the tools and the methods** that you need to prevent injuries in your clients. I will reveal EVERYTHING to you. However, the principles taught in this video are what **YOU NEED** to understand to be *successful with your injury prevention efforts...*

I have one request of you. I have dedicated my life to mastering these strategies, perfecting these methods and crafting these programs so that you can make a difference with injury prevention.

You're going to reach **levels of success you never dreamed possible** once you implement these methods, strategies and blueprint. You will impact a sea of people if you do what I'm sharing with you.

My request is that you please **SHARE THESE PRINCIPLES with the coaches you are influencing**. When we all work together, we can create a real and lasting change.

"Let's be SMARTT® - Let's do this together"

Injury Prevention Lessons
from The Dog Whisperer

"I'm a man of instinct" - All human beings have strong instincts when it comes to things like safety or not feeling very well, yet when it comes to movement, the industry teaches us our clients are doing it badly and that they need us to "correct it"...which is simply not true.

"The power of intention is very important" - Injuries are NOT the responsibility of fitness coaches, so working with our clients with the intention of "fixing" them is leading us into VERY hot water!

"Don't be afraid to dream big" - Fitness coaches have the power to play the lead role in the fight against injuries and change the face of the industry for good - if we work together

"I don't see failing" - If we focus on what our clients are doing wrong, we teach them to think that they aren't good enough or that they should trust our say so, rather than their own bodies. This creates HUGE problems for us.

"Claim what you want" - Find ways to help your clients achieve what they truly want...even when they can't tell you what that is

"Don't work against mother nature" - It's a fight you definitely won't win! Work WITH nature to create easier, faster solutions

"Calmness is the conversation to gain trust" - Getting caught up in our clients' injury problems, symptoms and pain only distracts us from the real issues at hand. Step back and you'll see more clearly.

"To know when to apply certain energy is key" - Any fool can copy movements and repeat explanations they may have heard, but to truly UNDERSTAND what you're doing and why, when it comes to improving movement, is the real skill that will change your clients lives and your coaching practices

"The less I think, the more I connect" - Using logic to test an infinite number of muscle restriction combinations takes too long. Remove the logic and allow your clients to feel, explore and experiment to get to the root cause quicker.

Once you're all set up

Your Job is to Keep the Injury Gremlins at Bay... and Have Fun Doing It!

The 5 Steps of Injury Prevention

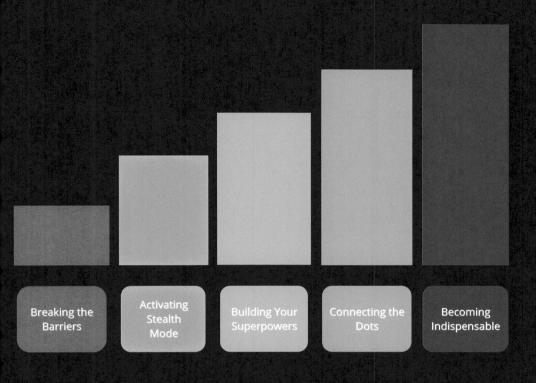

These 5 Steps Will Take Your Coaching to A Level That Others Can't Even Imagine...

Breaking the Barriers

Creating Deeper Connections

Taking the Strain
Resistance is NOT Your Clients' Fault!

Before you can start with any injury prevention intervention, it's **important that we know EXACTLY** what the conversation is that's going on inside your clients' heads, the conversation we're trying to have with them...and more importantly... **the DISCONNECT between the two**!

In order to avoid injuries effectively, we need to get feedback from our clients about what's been happening since we saw them last – even if we're restricted to asking our group at the start of each session to indicate if they have any injuries we should know about. But more often than not, we don't get the information we need to be able to best help them, because they are either unable or unwilling to give it, or they just don't see the relevance.

It's no good simply accepting this and when they get injured (which they will), blaming them because they didn't tell us...and we can't exactly spend hours digging into their previous medical history either, so how can we get around this?

Firstly, **we need to know who they are** (so we can make better decisions):

- How old are they?
- Are they male or female?
- What sport are they involved with?
- What level do they participate at?
- How frequently do they train?
- What do they do for a living?
- What responsibilities do they have outside of training?
- How much stress are they under right now?

Even if you're coaching groups, you can make a few generalizations and work from there. For example, do you coach an under 11's girls hockey team, who are local league champions and most of whom are heading off to high school in the coming months?

Or do you coach a "young at heart" low impact fitness class a couple of times a week for retired men and women?

This might not seem important, but *each group of people will have different reasons that influence what information you are, or are not given, as a fitness coach.*

Your clients need you to meet them where they are when it comes to feedback. They will always give you the best answer they can so it's up to YOU to help them give you more if that's what you need.

To help you do that, here are four questions to ask yourself, and an example of them being answered by the "young at heart" group coach mentioned earlier:

1. What are they saying?

This group of retired men and women are telling me they feel fine with the exercises I'm giving them. Nobody mentioned any aches and pains when I asked them at the beginning, and nobody has identified that they are struggling.

Many coaches would accept this silence as being a good sign and continue with the session as planned. But when we explore the next question, you'll see the disconnect between them and you – and _it's the identification of this disconnect that will help you to take more effective action_.

2. What do they really mean?

Older people have a tendency to "not want to be a burden". Sometimes this can lead to them sacrificing what they want or need. If any of the clients in this group don't want to highlight problems for fear of being a burden or problem to someone, they will stay quiet.

They are also less likely to disclose information to us about issues that trigger painful memories, and they are MUCH more likely to put aches and pains down to old age – which means that they don't consider them to be a relevant factor since they live with these issues all day, every day.

Understanding people, even a group of people, for who they are and respecting their situation rather than prying into it is one of the <u>fastest ways to develop deeper relationships with your clients</u> because they feel like you truly understand them, which _increases their trust and rapport with you_.

3. What's stopping them/getting in their way?

False beliefs about creating problems, worry about causing more damage than good, being perceived as "weak" or "frail" (which can have life-changing implications), previous surgery (the likelihood of this is much higher in older people)

Once you have identified some of the limiting factors, you'll know EXACTLY what steps to take to help your clients, giving them confidence and you <u>the opportunity to alter your practices</u> if they have the potential to make your clients feel worse.

4. How can I help them break through this?

Find opportunities to turn their negatives into positives, create activities that are challenging yet achievable, create activities that remove their fears.

Putting someone's fears to rest is a powerful thing to do and, in many cases, it can be life changing. It makes them feel like they can take on the world...and that's all because of YOU – so, can you imagine how they would feel if you did all that WITHOUT them having to voice their fears out loud? Taking the time to consider your actions **<u>gives you this power for every person in every session you coach.</u>**

Step #1 - Breaking the Barriers
Changing Your Language

Changing your language is perhaps the simplest thing you can do to break through the barriers and develop deep and long-lasting connections with your clients...and it's FREE!

Visit http://bit.ly/preventin60 to see it in action!

Steps For You to Follow
for Changing Your Language

Simple Tips for You to Implement with Your Clients

 Be less prescriptive. **Use feelings and mental imagery** so they start to connect emotionally with the movement. Tying a movement to a feeling <u>makes it easy to recreate quickly</u>

 Encourage exploration & curiosity. The position or movement might not be technically correct but will **help them to experience what feels good or not** - which means they can <u>tell you about it more easily</u>

 Use what you see to guide variety. Everyone follows instructions differently, so use the differences you see to encourage new ways of moving in your clients. **You don't need to have all the answers as a fitness coach!**

 Keep things positive. Your clients are usually trying their best (and if not there's usually a deeper reason for it that has nothing to do with you). Telling them that they're doing it wrong or moving badly won't help. Instead, <u>ask them to "try it like this"</u>

Seeing the Matrix

(The Secret Ingredient)

You'll never see the world the same way again!

 You're going to see the hidden opportunities for you to help your clients without them ever mentioning problems they're having. This <u>shows you understand them</u>, shows you as an expert and **builds the trust and rapport straight away**

 You're going to see your guidelines as a coach in a whole new light, so you can **deepen your expertise in the field you already love** AND develop an entirely new weapon in your arsenal too!

 You are going to know how to **get results that other coaches struggle to even imagine**, simply by coaching your regular sessions

 You're going to establish yourself as **someone other professionals want to work with**

 You're going to be identified as someone **your clients and their friends want to work with**

 You're going to be able to see how to EASILY **keep your clients in consistent patterns of training**, without the disruption of injury

Seeing the Matrix
Builds Confidence & Excitement

Jim - Functional Movement Practitioner

This course has blown apart everything I thought I knew about stretching, and how I can make a valid contribution to injury prevention without overstepping my role as a coach. Super informative and challenging (in a good way)!

Paul - Triathlon Coach

WOW! What an insightful course! It has given me a very different view of the tools I have at my disposal and I'm excited to see where it takes me!

Jacqui

World Age group Triathlon Champion & Coach

I thought I was pretty clued up about mobility - well, how wrong I was!

Sarah has created a fun, interesting and very informative course that leaves you excited about implementing new and effective ideas.

I would recommend this course to any coach wanting to incorporate more mobility into their sessions.

Whether you're new to mobility or a seasoned pro, you've NEVER seen anything like this before!

Seeing the Matrix
Keeps You Coaching

The Industry Wants to Turn You into a "Mini-Therapist"!

But the REAL magic is what happens when we can CLEARLY see how to BLEND these skills into <u>every single movement</u> your client makes...no injury knowledge required!

This **unique approach** will do EXACTLY that and will make your <u>coaching skills your TRUE superpower!</u>

"Be Excellent to Each Other"

 See beyond the words. In many situations, **words don't adequately describe** how someone is feeling or what they're thinking. Learn to look for the real meaning behind what's being said

 Make life **as easy as possible** for your clients to do, or give you, what you need to help them

 Keep your language simple. People have got enough to think about these days without adding copious amounts of teaching points that your clients will only remember one or two of anyway. This will help them focus on you and your session instead of worrying about work or family life.

 Keep your language positive. Build your clients' sense of achievement so they feel good about what they've done. They'll be berating themselves enough if they didn't do as well as they'd hoped, and if they are, it's easy for them to take even the smallest negative from you to heart. Keeping your language positive will change their belief from "I can't" to "I can" - or even better, "I did". That's what gets results!

 THE MOST IMPORTANT TACTIC – **Don't blame your client** for what the industry has created in them. I have a whole section on this in the coming page

Don't Blame Your Clients for the Industry's Failings

Here's how to gain trust and rapport

I'm going to make the whole process of preventing injuries very EASY for you. However, before I do, I want you to know that your **BIGGEST goal** when you work with clients is to *filter out the noise*.

Become an observer first!

This is how you discover what's REALLY happening. A client can tell you one thing when their body is clearly saying another. If you can filter out the noise, you'll get to the REAL problem, dealing with what the client says, what they really mean and the issues with the body, all at the same time!

AMAZING RIGHT?

So, it's important that you get this right.

Let me tell you where most coaches get this wrong. The fitness industry has been teaching our clients (through OUR words and actions) that they have bad technique, movement dysfunctions, where they "should" be feeling stretches and how hard to train for so long now that our clients have completely lost all connection with their own bodies...yet we rely on THEIR words to inform our decisions.

If you are doing any of these things, STOP!

- ✓ Adapting your sessions based on what your clients SAY
- ✓ Listening not observing
- ✓ Asking lots of questions
- ✓ Talking AT not talking WITH
- ✓ Trying to lead your clients to the verbal feedback you need
- ✓ Focusing on the client's problems
- ✓ Waiting to start the session until you have all the info you need

Here's the RIGHT Way to Do This!

Step 1: Understand that what you hear isn't really what's wrong

Here's an example:

"I didn't have time this week". Time is a classic excuse that very rarely is the REAL problem.

Step 2: DON'T accept the first thing you hear

Many coaches would jump in at this point to try to make the sessions shorter because they're focused on what the client SAID. Instead, ask an open-ended question like "what changed?". This gives your client the chance to explain more/get things off their chest...but DON'T be drawn into this, just let them talk. Humans have become too reliant on words, but **our clients need to be AWARE of their problems before they can explain them to us**

Step 3: WATCH them move

Get your client doing something simple like walking, but not for the sake of it... observe them as they move. How are they holding themselves? Does their movement look comfortable? Do they FEEL stressed to you? Are they moving less comfortably than usual?

Bodies will reveal clues about problems long before our clients can explain them to us, we just need to learn to look a little bit closer.

For example, if they walk around like they've got the weight of the world on their shoulders, or they're talking so much that you think they might burst, it's likely that they have a lot of stress in their lives right now. Your client might not recognise this, but **using these clues to get beyond the words shows your client that you really understand them**

Step 4: Prioritise what you SEE

Take your observations first, then layer on what the client told you to determine your actions.

For example, if you observe your client looking more slumped than usual, they look and feel like they've lost the usual spring in their step and they've told you that things have been super busy at work, you might think that a slower paced, gentle stretching style session might be most appropriate for them... but <u>STILL don't take action yet</u>!

Step 5: Ask them what they want and GIVE them it!

It might sound obvious, but never assume you know what's best for your client. You might recognise that they need to release the tension, but that can come in many forms. Let them tell you what they want, then GIVE IT TO THEM (with a healthy dose of what they need too!).

Just forging ahead with a gentle stretch session when your client would much prefer to punch something would only show them that you don't understand them. They might feel a bit better after stretching, but they probably wouldn't enjoy the session.

The simple act of asking them beforehand, allows you to give them what they want and THAT shows them exactly how awesome you really are...but when we layer on what you know they need too, that takes you to a whole new level!

That's it! It really is that EASY! Once you become good at this, you can adapt ANY session to give your clients exactly what they want AND what they need!

In fact, on the next page there's a video that just shows you so you can see for yourself!

"Eyes, Ears, Ask, Give" in Action
Watch how this works - LIVE!

I went LIVE in our Facebook group to demonstrate how this amazing process works. You will see how I am able to prioritise body language over words, involve the client and then deliver EXACTLY what they wanted – and more!

Listen to the feedback I got at the end of the session!
Click the button below to watch this video...GET READY!

Visit
http://bit.ly/bestinjuryadvice
to see it in action!

You need compassion and insight

 Master my *"Eyes, Ears, Ask, Give"* strategy. It works so VERY WELL. Eventually you'll be able to transition into seeing what the client needs way before they say anything, like you saw me do on the video

 Make sure you **practice it every day.** It's a challenge but once you get good at this, you will LOVE it! It can then become a cornerstone of your coaching that helps you to deliver outstanding results... FAST!

 Make sure you **know your coaching boundaries** ahead of time. You should always know whether you're working inside of your remit or not (and it's amazing how many coaches are venturing into dangerous territory without even realizing it). That's why I created the **Injury Prevention Decoded online training.**

 You're going to learn more about **practical movement solutions** in the next section. It's there that you'll realise how all of this comes into play

 Don't assume that you know best! I'm telling you - this is the biggest mistake I see coaches making when they try to master injury prevention. Don't do this. You have the secret now – USE IT!

 People LOVE having what THEY want. Learn to make this a habit. **It's the BEST way to form a connection** so you can *build the trust and rapport with your clients* (even in a group!). GIVE THEM IT! Serve your people!

 Make sure you're **prepared for a variety of situations** and you'll be able to pivot quickly, without even missing a beat – which will make you look like a rockstar!

Practice "Eyes, Ears, Ask, Give" **every single day** (even if you're not coaching!). You'll get super-attuned. Don't give up!

 Don't assume you know best! Human bodies are way more than the muscles and bones that they're made up of. Every single client has had unique experiences in their lives that can lead (or may have already led) to any number of problems. Treat them like the unique and complex beings that they are.

 Stay true to coaching. **Always know your coaching boundaries** and how you can BEST USE THEM to help your clients prevent injury

 Invite your clients to **have input and give feedback on multiple occasions** throughout your sessions. It truly gives them a personal touch and creates a stronger bond between you (yes, even if it's a group)

 Share feedback from one group or client with another (anonymously of course). It can **give them ideas of what to say** if they're struggling and shows that others are getting results

 Always encourage clients to tell you how they feel at the end of your session. It'll help you improve and **show them that you care.**

Step #2
Activating Stealth Mode
Using Your EXISTING Coaching Skills

Forget Everything You Know About
Mobility and Injury Prevention

How to Prevent Injury Without Spending Time on It. Do This Right and You Won't Even Need to Have Mobility in Your Sessions

Please listen to me closely. So many of my clients come to me with pre-conceived ideas of what mobility is. Many of them have spent hours studying the industry's "best practices".

That's what they've been told they have to do to stay within their role as a coach. I've seen, used and even taught many of these practices over the years and they can get results. They often use fancy gadgets and the latest science...

But there's one little problem...

YOU HAVE TO STOP COACHING TO DO THEM!

If I asked 10, 100 or even 1000 coaches if they related to this, I'd be willing to bet that about 95% of them would absolutely agree (well, you always get a few that don't).

We have entered an era of simplicity and expectation

If you follow the process I am showing you in this guide, you will make your clients as bulletproof as it's humanly possible to make them when it comes to avoiding injury...but you have to follow everything I am telling you.

When you do follow this process, you won't even need a "mobility" section of your session. You might not even need to ask your clients to spend any of their own time on it. You'll simply get on with delivering your sessions, like you used to before mobility became trendy.

Session structure has been a standard way for decades. Yet we can make it into the most powerful injury prevention tool you've ever seen. You will OVER DELIVER for your clients and they will know that you have their best interests at heart!

Are you getting this? I hope you're having a huge lightbulb moment right now. I call this your **"Fitness Coaching Superpower"**. This is the way that you are truly going to make a difference to your clients' lives.

But it requires...

Consistency and Commitment

Have the Consistency and COMMITMENT

Please hear what I am saying. The BEST way to build deep and lasting connections with your clients is to commit to doing what they need FOR them.

A triathlon coach friend of mine once said something to me years ago, and I've never forgotten it...

Triathlon coaching is about much more than just swim, bike, run

And the same can be said for any sport or fitness coaching. When we coach people, we're dealing with much more than just the exercise inside of the session. We're responsible for all the extra elements that KEEP them training too, like:

Warming Up

Cooling Down

Stretching

Recovering from training

You need to take advantage of the most overlooked parts of your session, so you can take the pressure off your clients.

Focus EVERY Element on Injury Prevention!

✓ Warming Up

✓ Cooling Down

✓ Stretching

✓ Recovering from training

(and I don't just mean raising & lowering body temperature!)

The Challenge
Put Your Money Where Your Mouth is...

I was challenged to create a warm up, cool down and recovery day routine for a group of runners over 40 - this is what happened

The Warm Up...

Industry Standard

Activity: Gentle Jogging

Duration: 5 mins

Aim: Raise Heart Rate and Body Temperature

Outcome: Clients feel warmer but joints often still felt stiff, especially over 40 years old

Clients' Attention on Session: Low - they just want to get out running, they believe they'll warm up while running

Total Minutes Preventing Injury: 5   Effectiveness:

SMARTT® Methods

Activity: Hip Preparation 3M Flow™ Sequence

Duration: 5 mins

Aim: Open Hips, Improve Shock Absorption, Raise HR & Increase Body Temp

Outcome: Clients feel warm, joints feel looser and ready to run

Clients' Attention on Session: High - they are focused on the session from the start

Total Minutes Preventing Injury: 5   Effectiveness:

Industry Standard

Activity: Gentle Jogging & Stretching

Duration: 0 - 10 mins

Aim: Lower Heart Rate and Body Temperature & Restore Muscle Length

Outcome: Clients cool down but stretching often feels like a struggle. They often feel exhausted by the session and sore for a few days after.

Clients' Attention on Session: Low - they think they cool down by walking to the shower.

Total Minutes Preventing Injury: 0 - 10   **Effectiveness:**

SMARTT® Methods

Activity: Hip Improvement 3M Flow™ Sequence

Duration: 10 mins

Aim: Improve Hip Movement in All Directions, Decrease HR & Body Temp

Outcome: Clients manage movements easily, feel tired but relaxed after session and not sore in next few days

Clients' Attention on Session: High - they find the movements fun yet challenging

Total Minutes Preventing Injury: 10   **Effectiveness:**

The Recovery Session
This is Most Commonly Where Clients "Go Rogue" or "Off Plan"

Industry Standard

Activity: Total Rest or Light Active Recovery

Duration: 0 - 30 mins

Aim: Give body a rest from strain of regular activity

Outcome: Clients often feel rested but quickly feel fatigued when resuming exercise

Clients' Attention on Session: Low - Clients don't like not training, they often can't help pushing too hard on light activity or thinking that it's an opportunity to catch up on sessions they may have missed during the week

Total Minutes Preventing Injury: 0 - 30   **Effectiveness:**

SMARTT® Methods

Activity: Hip Deep Dive 3M Flow™ Sequence

Duration: 30 mins

Aim: Improve Hip Movement in All Directions & Unwind Twist in Muscle Fibres to Increase Blood Flow and Help Flush Toxins

Outcome: Clients feel rested and ready to train again

Clients' Attention on Session: High - they like having something useful to do when they're not training. They "go rogue" or "off-plan" less and make better use of their "down" time.

Total Minutes Preventing Injury: 30   **Effectiveness:**

Overall Comparison

Over 2 Hours Without Trying!

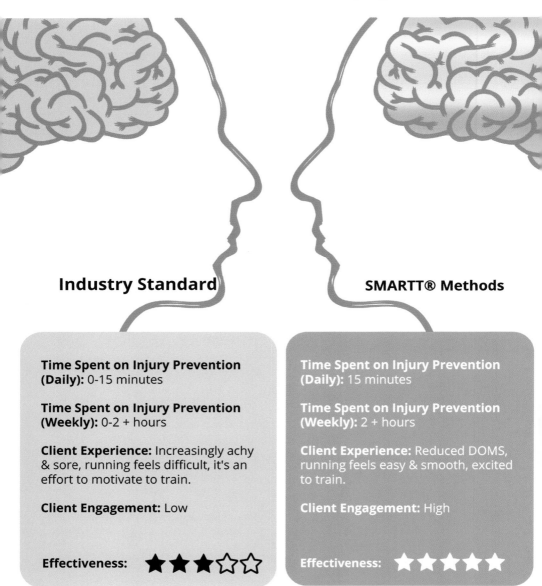

Industry Standard

Time Spent on Injury Prevention (Daily): 0-15 minutes

Time Spent on Injury Prevention (Weekly): 0-2 + hours

Client Experience: Increasingly achy & sore, running feels difficult, it's an effort to motivate to train.

Client Engagement: Low

Effectiveness: ★★★☆☆

SMARTT® Methods

Time Spent on Injury Prevention (Daily): 15 minutes

Time Spent on Injury Prevention (Weekly): 2 + hours

Client Experience: Reduced DOMS, running feels easy & smooth, excited to train.

Client Engagement: High

Effectiveness: ★★★★★

Your EXISTING Training Time is DUAL Purpose
Which MASSIVELY Increases Value

Now We're Creating a REAL Injury Prevention Solution!

Here's just a few examples of what they're achieving...

Chris Yates

Chris is a Personal Trainer specialising in working with the elderly, those with complex health issues, and learning difficulties.

Simply by blending these injury prevention methods into his regular exercise sessions, he has been able to help his clients build vital confidence in themselves and motivation to continue with their fitness despite their health challenges.

Like Margaret, a 69 year old client of his who loved attending her Zumba classes, until they began to trigger her arthritis. Her motivation to exercise began to slip away because of the pain, which didn't help her type 2 diabetes. Chris created an appropriate warm up routine which helped mobilise her joints so they were less painful. This has been the trigger to give her the enthusiasm she needed to get back into regular exercising and keep her diabetes under control.

Jacqui is a World and European Age Group World Champion Triathlete who works full time, coaches part-time and tries to fit her own training in too!

She was struggling to find time to fit in her own mobility training, but since she's been teaching and demonstrating this new style of warming up and cooling down, she's found that she doesn't actually need to spend time on her own mobility at all!

Jacqui Phillips

So not only is she helping to prevent injuries with her own clients, but she's preventing her own too!

They've Even Been Changing...
Their Own Lives!

Here's just a few examples of what they're achieving...

Shirley Fox

Shirley is a Pilates Teacher who enjoys keeping herself fit doing triathlons. She teaches upwards of 20 Pilates sessions per week but she says she felt almost ashamed that she was teaching a style of fitness that was supposed to prevent injury yet she was injured herself.

Since she's been blending these injury prevention methods into what she teaches, she's not struggling with her own injuries anymore and many of her clients (who are in their 60s & 70s) are commenting on how much looser their bodies feel!

Martin is an outdoor adventure instructor who dislocated his shoulder white water rafting a few years ago.

Since then, he has struggled to demonstrate certain moves in a kayak and has felt apprehensive of using his arm in certain positions, which has severely limited his ability to demonstrate activities.

Martin Higgins

He has been using these injury prevention techniques to improve his own range of movement in his shoulder, and those of his clients so that he can demonstrate confidently again and prevent his clients from suffering the same fate that he did!

What's the Secret?

Ultimately getting more results for your tribe...

I'm going to introduce you to a concept that will FOREVER change everything about your coaching. It's a concept that I have mastered, not just with my students, but also in life.

Are you ready for that concept?

STEALTH MODE!

"Taking place in secret"

That's the official definition from yourdictionary.com. I like to refer to it as **"gift-wrapping"**. In other words, we are going to make it VERY EASY and fun to take action with their mobility.

That action could be something as simple as adding movement to the stretches they already know and use at home. By the way, that is one of the **most effective ways** to help your clients get started helping themselves when it comes to preventing injury.

They're MUCH More Likely...
to Do Things They LIKE Doing

Like when you try to get kids to eat vegetables...

and you whizz them in a blender to make a deliciously thick and tasty pasta sauce

or you make the pizza base out of cauliflower

or you make their favourite brownies with sweet potato!

I Created My Own Solution...

Pretty incredible right? There was **no such system on the planet** so I had to create it myself.

I wanted a system that allowed coaches to **give clients what they WANTED** (get on with training) at the same time as delivering what they NEEDED (injury prevention).

I wanted to be able to **get results in a few minutes, not hours**!

I wanted to be able to **use these methods anywhere,** without equipment

I wanted **ANYBODY of any age or movement capability** to be able to use these methods

I wanted to be able to **use movements that were easy to do**, not have clients worry that they would be doing them wrong

I wanted **big groups to be able to use the same movements** yet still customise them to suit their own needs

I wanted coaches to be able to become a **big part of the injury conversation** – regardless of their level of understanding

I wanted people to **stop having to pay out endless amounts for ongoing treatment** or injury management sessions

I wanted **upcoming stars to be able to fulfil their potential**, not drop out due to injury

I wanted to **END the inevitability of sporting injuries in the world**

So, I had to create my own solution, and you're going to hear about the solution later on in the chapters.

Say Goodbye to All of This...

We'll talk more about this system in the later chapters.

Just know that it's everything you've been looking for...

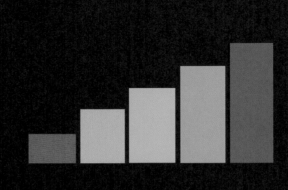

Step #3
Building Your Superpowers
Time to Skyrocket Your Clients' Results

This is How Your Clients Become Injury- Resistant

It's time to get specific!

Now your clients are being consistent with their mobility, it's time to take your coaching (and their results) to a level that other coaches struggle to imagine.

We're going to take all your clients' technique and performance problems away – without spending hours on drills or endless repetition!

If we want our clients to become resilient...

We Have to Stop Being Generic!

When you follow this process, you will have already started helping your clients to feel better in their movements. Very little technique specific time will be necessary.

Breaking skills down into individual drills is optional, but not really needed to:

✓ Build Strength

✓ Protect Joints

✓ Improve Technique

✓ Improve Movement Efficiency

✓ Reduce Wear & Tear on Joints

If you do this right...
Your clients won't need to spend time on their technique problems.

Drills and repetition are for those people who don't understand how nature works or haven't appreciated their clients for the individuals that they are.

if you do it right...

Most coaches think that <u>adding weights to movements</u> like squats will protect their clients' joints from injury – and it will to a certain extent.

The problem is, that traditional strength training uses movements that must be ***done the "correct" way*** (which means high volumes of repetition), and progression is measured through the amount of weight a person can lift safely.

This excessive repetition, at the expense of other ways of moving the joints and under increasing weight, means that ***we aren't building resilience into our clients' joints***, we're simply building stiffness around the joint so it can't move anywhere else!

And to make things worse, in most cases, ***not enough consideration is given to the client's existing individual movement habits***. So, this stiffness is built on top of existing issues as the <u>coaches focus on getting the exercise movement "right"</u>.

At first, this stiffness seems to support the joints, but soon, those underlying individual movement habits start to show through the cracks and **they start to create problems** – especially when joints are being asked to move in different ways all of a sudden, like a runner tripping over a tree root when running through the woods, or the weight slipping at the bottom of a back squat, for example.

I have lost count of the number of clients I've dealt with ***who've developed pain*** after strength training in this way, so pay attention to what I'm about to tell you when it comes to strength training!

I've spent over 30 years in the fitness industry, participating, coaching, rehabilitating and treating injury. I've seen strength training techniques develop and trends come and go, so I know a thing or two about the impact that current strength training techniques have on the human body!

If they can bend...They Won't Break!

 Add as much variety as possible to every single strength training exercise. It is very common for me to add at least six variations in every single session. **I've identified over 200 possible variations for any given exercise.**

 Make sure you identify the underlying movement issue that your client is struggling with and **base all your programming around it**

 Industry standard "correct" techniques are good when you're trying to compete or perform assessments, but they are not great for preventing injury. **There is NO WAY to cater for individual needs when you're always looking for "correct".** You will however make small improvements to technique and performance.

 When you focus your strength training around your client's individual needs and combine it with variety of movement, you will **BLOW up your client's results** and you'll help protect them from injury

 I have a strategy called the **"Silent Performance Gremlin Eliminator"** which is going to *double or triple your clients' performance results* once you start using it

 Traditional strength training methods are losing popularity. I'm now going to introduce you to my **"Super Results Generation" Formula**

Introducing...

The Super Results Generation Formula

What if You Could Improve Your Clients' Technique and Performance FASTER & With LESS EFFORT?

Like these guys and gals...

"This has encouraged me to broaden my horizons and think outside the box rather than use the standard, one glove fits all approach. Very refreshing"

Fiona Hoare - Triathlon Coach

"This has given me the tools and confidence to improve my clients performances in ways that are only ever hinted at by mainstream coaching and physiotherapy. The results are fast, effective and life changing, not just in athletic performance"

Martin Higgins - Outdoor Adventure Coach

"This approach should be the cornerstone of fitness coaching education. I love how my thinking can get straight to the heart of the problem without overwhelming or confusing my clients."

Margaret Sills - Triathlon Coach

This is going to give you super loyal, consistent and injury-resilient clients – even if they're brand new to you!

 From the start, make it clear your clients are going to **achieve a specific result!** *(Make swimming / running / squatting feel easier/faster/more powerful)*

 Set out a 30-Day timeframe to deliver this result. You might not need that long, but this timeframe gives you time to show **just how effective your coaching is**

 You include a weekly coaching call to help you **engage with your client** and keep your programming on track to deliver maximum results

 One of the most effective ways to get results is to **do it with them**. Follow along videos are a great way to do this, **saving you time** while your <u>client feels more connected to you</u>

 Focus every warm up, cool down, recovery day, skill acquisition and strength training session within the 30 days **around your client's individual movement habits** and variety of movement, then ask them if they are satisfied with the outcome. If so, ask them if they'd like to continue training with you

 Make sure you deploy the "Silent Performance Gremlin Eliminator" strategy during this 30-day period. It will **double or triple your clients' results.**

Case Study - Chris Yates

When I first started working with "Yasmine", she was struggling with persistently tight hamstrings and a numbness in her little toe that was preventing her from walking very far, driving and doing other tasks of normal daily life.

She wasn't sleeping very well, couldn't run and struggled to relax but was using exercise to manage her stress levels.

During my initial assessment it would have been easy to miss her subtle movement restrictions. She had a good posture, good alignment in standing and a comfortable gait. She also had reasonable balance, but using the "Silent Performance Gremlins Eliminator" strategy, I was able to identify two main areas that were likely to be contributing to her symptoms and restricting her daily life.

"Yasmine" was happy attending group classes for her main exercise sessions, so I created a series of warm-up, cool-down and recovery day routines for her to follow that helped her to deal specifically with her individual issues.

At first, "Yasmine" was simply doing the classes because she felt that they were helping, but when we started dialling into her specific issues, she noticed that she'd been over-exerting herself and was able to make the informed decision to switch her approach to something more suitable to her.

Since her problems have been ongoing for a while, she is also seeing a Physio and undergoing tests from the doctor. At first I was a bit nervous working within a team like this, but I quickly realised that we were all working on differing, yet complementary approaches which gave me the confidence to continue.

Within the course of her 30-day programme, "Yasmine" is now making more appropriate decisions regarding the intensity of her fitness, she's sleeping much better, she can drive her car, walk and live her daily life without discomfort, and she feels that the numbness in her foot is improving. Running beyond 1km is a work in progress and she's still waiting for her next doctor's appointment.

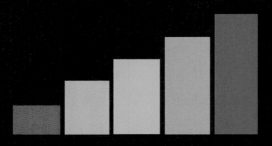

Step #4
Connecting the Dots
Stepping into Your Full Potential

Providing Results = More Revenue

I don't know how to stress this more than I already have. You need to have consistency and commitment to build a really strong coaching identity and a tribe of consistent clients

I can GUARANTEE that if you do EVERYTHING I outlined in this guide, you're going to be in that position. Show your clients that you can get results, and then do it again, and again, and again!

Here's what's so amazing, if you're willing to go all in...

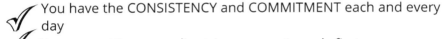 You have the CONSISTENCY and COMMITMENT each and every day

 You are putting your clients' movement needs first

 You demonstrate that you are head and shoulders above every other coach out there

 You are providing so much more than just training requirements

 You are mastering the art of preventing injury

You get your clients' results faster and easier than ever

You are positioning yourself as a trusted and respected professional in the eyes of other professionals

I CAN GUARANTEE THEY WILL BE THE MOST LOYAL AND CONSISTENT CLIENTS YOU'VE EVER HAD AND ***YOU WON'T HAVE THE HASSLE OF FINDING NEW CLIENTS*** – THEY'LL START FINDING YOU!

Connecting the Dots
To Take Your Coaching to the Next Level!

There are 3 factors of pain/injury...yet most only focus on one or two...

When I refer to "connecting the dots", I'm talking about understanding the factors that combine to create injury and **your place in the middle of it.** Most coaches won't ever reach this level of understanding but they're missing a HUGE opportunity.

I have identified **3 main factors that converge** when it comes to pain/injuries and fitness training:

> **1. Body** – This is what the majority of the industry focuses on, but it is not the complete picture. What's happening with muscles, bones, connective tissue and the tightness within the body is only part of the story

> **2. Mind** – How a client feels about their pain and/or previous pain is a powerful influence on the third factor

> **3. Action** – What is happening in the client's body and mind will dictate what actions they will and won't take when it comes to their training.

Understanding each of these factors, how they converge into the motivation, confidence and performance of your clients will take your coaching to a level that most other coaches won't even consider – and that **puts you at a MASSIVE advantage!**

There are 3 factors of pain/injury...yet most only focus on one or two...

Body:
Physical Therapists, Bodyworkers and Specialist Fitness Trainers focus here

Mind:
Behavourial Therapists, Psychotherapists and Counsellors focus on this

Action:
Sports and Fitness Coaches focus on this, regardless of their level of understanding of injury.

Specialist Fitness Trainers & Physical Therapists try to connect the body with action but often exclude the mind component **which results in limited or temporary results.**

When we start connecting the dots, we **take care to understand** what other professionals are trying to achieve, the toll of pain (or even the experience of previous pain) on our clients and **what we can do to ease the situation for everyone involved.**

This is how you stand head and shoulders above the crowd of other sports and fitness coaches

Fitness industry standard courses that deal with injuries drag coaches away from coaching and into hands-on treatment. This is NOT that.

You have already seen in this guide, just how much faster and easier you can improve your clients' movement, technique and performance by following these steps. Now it's time to show everyone just how capable you are...without becoming something you're not!

This means understanding where other professionals are coming from so we can see how you can help them, and you can demonstrate how:

 Medical professionals don't need to spend time explaining details to you (which shows you understand them)

 You're not trying to duplicate their work or disrupt it (which helps build trust)

 You are complementary to them (which increases referrals to you)

 You can help clients easily understand what is happening in their bodies (shows knowledge & expertise without the jargon)

 Increases compliance from clients (which makes you look good in the eyes of other professionals)

One of the biggest barriers to successful injury prevention is the technical jargon. It's confusing, and sometimes daunting for clients and puts many coaches off even trying to get involved.

But one of the most important things you need to understand about the medical language is that it's only necessary for the medical professionals – not you!

As coaches, it's helpful for us to understand what it means, but it's not what will ultimately drive our actions. We use a system that helps us to keep our focus simple and our actions effective. It's what I call the "Whole Human Method".

We will get into this method, but first let me tell you a quick story about how we end up here...

15 Years of Undiagnosed PTSD

In 2001 I was physically assaulted in my own home. My back was so bruised that I could hardly stand upright and a black horizontal line highlighted on my skin where each of my vertebrae was.

As a young 20 something year-old, recently graduated from university, I'd been out drinking with some friends earlier in the evening and had gone home to bed. I don't remember exactly what happened, but I do remember being in my pj's in my housemate's bedroom being hit by her partner.

It was no secret that I didn't like the woman she was seeing. She was a bully and controlling and I'd made it clear to my housemate that I didn't want her in the house. Yet here she was standing over me in my own house repeatedly punching me while all I could do was curl over in an attempt to protect myself.

I still don't know to this day why I was in my housemate's bedroom or why her partner was there, but I had this feeling in my gut that somehow, I had brought this "fight" on myself. I was so filled with shame that I didn't tell a soul. The only people that knew were my housemate and a friend, who offered to take me to her martial arts classes.

Over the next couple of weeks, my body healed, and I began to regain some of my confidence through the martial arts training. A few months later I moved away from that town and never looked back.

I didn't think about the assault much over the next few years, but within a year or two, I tore my hamstring and began struggling with back pain.

I didn't know then what I know now about injuries, so I was relying on other people to help me deal with them. It was then that someone offered to do a spinal adjustment. Unfortunately, this, combined with a different treatment I was having for my hamstring, strained the ligaments in my spine and I was in agony for a few weeks.

After this settled, I began developing little nagging problems in my knee, hip and shoulder but despite trying many conventional treatments, my body seemed far too sensitive to cope with any of them and afterwards I always ended up feeling worse than before!

I've always been fit and active my whole life but around 2012, I started noticing that after intense exercise, my body would just shake like I'd had too much caffeine, and it would take ages to settle.

Gradually, as my work stress increased, this reaction to intense exercise got worse, so I ended up not really training at all.

It felt like nobody understood what was happening and I felt like I was going to training but not really putting any effort in, which made me miserable.

It's not surprising, given that all this was happening to me, that the focus of my entire career has been injuries, and during the same timeframe, I'd progressed from being a Fitness Instructor, to a Personal Trainer, to a Rehabilitation Assistant in the NHS, to a Corrective Exercise Specialist, to a Soft-Tissue Therapist in an attempt to help people like me who seemed to be suffering from persistent and nagging injury issues.

But it wasn't until I spoke to what seemed like the umpteenth therapist about my injuries that it was suggested that my body's extreme reaction to treatment wasn't normal and that it was similar to those suffering from PTSD.

This new information changed everything for me.

It helped me understand why my body wasn't tolerating high intensity exercise, why I'd struggled with all these nagging injuries and why I was being so sensitive to treatment.

But, not just that, it also helped me understand smaller behavioural changes I'd begun to notice, like being completely demotivated by fitness coaches shouting, or digging my heels in and refusing to add more weight to my bar in group class (and almost having a stand-up argument about it in front of everyone).

I'd even become super-sensitive to changes in atmosphere – to the point where I knew a fight was brewing in a pub before it happened and insisting to my friends that we must leave immediately.

I'll admit, I've kept this information about myself under lock and key for many years, and even now, sharing this with you isn't the easiest thing for me to do, but I hope it highlights just the kind of deeply personal, and hugely relevant information that our clients DON'T share with us as coaches.

We focus on the sport or movement patterns of our clients' bodies and sometimes, we're unknowingly expecting our clients' lack of motivation or inconsistencies to be something to do with our programming or some kind of physical issue.

If I was your client right now and you didn't know this about me (which is likely because I wouldn't have wanted to tell anyone, even you!), it's most likely that we'd be parting ways before long.

You'd likely get frustrated at my apparent lack of effort or inconsistent training patterns and I'd get demotivated by my own lack of progress.

At best, I might tag along at the back of a group exercise class, where I'm less likely to be noticed, slowly getting demoralised at my own inconsistent capabilities.

And even if you DID have this information about me as your client – what could you even do about it?

If my experience of my own injuries and over 15 years of coaching and treating other people with injuries has taught me anything, it's that the whole system is very fragmented – **and that's why it's not working!**

Each professional involved is responsible for their own specialty, and each of them is trying their best to improve the client's situation, given what they know.

The problem is, that the one person who knows least about the situation is the one that's being relied on for all the information...**the client!**

Our clients try their best to remember what they've been told by other professionals. They try to remember the technical jargon in the hope that it will make our lives as coaches, easier. But when it comes down to it, if they don't understand what they've bee told, **mistakes are easily made!**

I've lost count of the times a client has said to me something like "medial hamstring" and when I've asked them to point at where their pain is, they're pointing at their elbow or somewhere!

And if we add to that the fact that the fitness industry has us constantly reminding our clients that they move badly (by focusing on improving technique or using phrases like "dysfunctional"), or asking them to ignore what they're feeling – pushing them to do "jus one more" when they want to stop, it's hardly surprising that they don't trust themselve to make a decision about their own bodies.

But that leaves them in the horrible situation of having to coordinate two, three or even more professionals. Which is time consuming, tiring and sometimes confusing if those professionals have slightly conflicting ideas, or worse – no idea of what to do to help. An as a client once reminded me:

"I don't want to have to think, I just want _**one person**_ to tell me what to do!"

72

That's why I created my "Whole Human Method". I'm going to reveal that to you here shortly, but it reminds coaches of all levels to acknowledge that there are more powerful forces at play than we can ever comprehend, with each and every single one of our clients – and that we are in the BEST position to be able to do something to improve things, for everyone involved!

Just like fitness coaches, therapists also specialize in their area of interest. For some
of them, it's late-stage rehabilitation and branching out into exercise, but many of them HATE doing this with patients and would jump at the chance to hand their patients off to someone else who understands their treatment plan, so they don't have to spend ages explaining the ins-and-outs of each patient's case.

And in addition to this, therapists working on an emotional level with patients often
use exercise as a way to alleviate symptoms of anxiety and depression. Many of these therapists don't have the skills or the interest to support their clients with this either.

But YOU DO! You can be that ONE PERSON. That bridge supporting your clients in ALL aspects of their injury issues – without once treading on other professionals' toes or stopping the coaching that you love so much!

Enter...

The Whole Human Method

The Whole Human Method
3 Converging Factors

BODY   **MIND**   **ACTION**

Here's how this works. The goal of the Whole Human Method is to become the bridge between therapy (both physical and emotional) and your client.

Just because you become a bridge does not mean that you have to go and qualify in each discipline. Instead we understand what the goals of each discipline are, the language that they speak and translate it into what WE do as coaches. That way, we are complementing what each of these therapies is trying to achieve, not duplicating or disrupting them.

Bridging BODYwork means understanding what the physical therapist is trying to achieve with their hands-on soft-tissue treatment and translating it into non-painful movement. This helps your clients to build a positive experience about moving their bodies in ways that have previously caused them pain, which means helping to remove the emotional barriers that may be preventing their bodies from moving easily and which may be contributing to their levels of pain.

Bridging MINDwork means understanding that your clients may have lived through previous trauma or have high levels of anxiety that are limiting their abilities to achieve their fitness goals. Translating this understanding into non-painful movements that allow them to explore and gently push the boundaries of their own movement can help to re-frame the mind's reaction to being in certain positions or moving in certain ways that have previously caused pain or anxiety.

Complimenting other professionals in this way adds MASSIVE value to your services and it's at this point that all kinds of magical things start to happen. Not only do your clients get the straightforward, simple instruction they were desperate for, but their other professionals will start to notice the unusually big jumps in improvement that those clients are making between sessions.

When something out of the ordinary starts happening, questions start being asked, and YOU start to get noticed. Your results start to speak for themselves and – even though they may never have met or even spoken to you, referrals will start coming your way!

Your clients will no longer have the burden of having to relay complex technical information about their condition – I've even had clients say things like "I don't know how she does it, but all I'm doing is moving a bit like this and it's helping!"

I Created My Own Injury Prevention Solution

Are you starting to understand what's been created here? Everything has been created from a need in my own business and frustrations with the system as a whole.

My clients wanted ONE PERSON to tell them what to do. That way they didn't have the burden of having to relay technical messages or worry that they might not get some of it right.

I wanted to be able to pass my treatment clients onto a fitness coach who **understood what I was trying to do** and could HELP our mutual clients do more of it without replicating my treatment or disrupting it.

I wanted my clients' coaches to **understand the impact that the lingering effects of trauma was having on their bodies** and the programming implications that had. Particularly on the level of intensity of exercise that client could cope with.

I wanted my **clients to do more to help themselves outside of my treatment room**, and the BEST time to do that was when they were already doing something active.

I wanted **fitness coaches to stop being ignored** when it comes to the injury conversation and help them become the valuable piece of the puzzle that they are.

I wanted **any sports or fitness coach** to be able to make a safe and effective contribution to the injury process, *regardless of their level of certification*.

Finally I wanted a way for **ALL sports or fitness coaches to be able to communicate easily with medical professionals** to break down the barriers and get MILLIONS more caring individuals involved in helping clients avoid injuries...I mean, let's face it, nobody actually WANTS anyone to suffer with injuries do they?!

So, I had to create my own solution, and you're going to hear about this later on in the coming chapters.

MAKE SPORTING INJURIES THE EXCEPTION RATHER THAN THE RULE

We'll talk more about this solution in the later chapters. Just know that it is absolutely phenomenal!

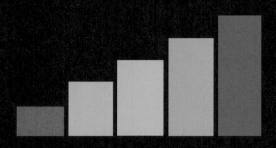

Step #5
Becoming Indispensable
Creating True Collaboration

Becoming Indispensable
Creating Your Ecosystem

This is where it all comes together

Look at everything you have learned. AMAZING STRATEGIES, right? You also learned about the different levels that mastering injury prevention can take you to.

I'm almost ready to give you a sneak peek into the suite of training I've created to show you how to achieve all this, but first I want to make sure you understand something.

All of these things we've covered:

 Truly understanding your clients

 Safeguarding yourself as a coach

 Exploiting overlooked areas of your session to maximise your clients' results

 Easily eliminating technique & performance problems

 Lightning fast assessments

 Becoming the communication bridge between other professionals and your clients

These are all things that we have been talking about in this guide. But to see this vision achieved in all its glory, we need clients and therapists to become part of the equation.

What if you and I could work side-by-side to help you create your own referral network? This would mean you would be connecting with the most appropriate complementary professionals and bringing MORE CLIENTS to you.

You could then work in wonderful harmony to make a HUGE difference to your clients' lives – and the best bit is that they would be EXACTLY the kinds of clients that you love working with! AMAZING, RIGHT?

The Communication Network
Collaboration = MASSIVE Results!

But...The Communication Network is NOT for Everyone

Only the most dedicated of coaches will want to join forces with other professionals to create a seamless collaboration environment, and that means that it won't be for everyone. But that DOESN'T mean that other coaches can't be included in the ecosystem of those who do.

True collaboration means **identifying the skills and abilities of everyone involved and creating a unique environment where they can ALL contribute**. When you have a simple way to communicate, your ecosystem can be in any location, anywhere in the world (providing you have a good internet connection!).

Developing connections like this is how you will become an indispensable part of your ecosystem, build and **future-proof your business!**

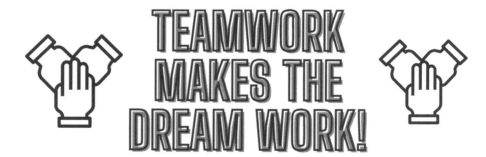

Introducing...

The SMARTT® Methods

by mostmotion.

The SMARTT® Methods are the ONLY approach a fitness coach needs to help prevent injury

In 2012 I began to realise that there wasn't really a way for me to take care of my clients through the entire injury process, from pain to it never coming back again. I wanted a way of helping my clients easily go through the entire process.

What used to take months, I can now help my clients do in a few days. The only reason why is because of the system I built for my own business. It's the fastest and simplest path to results you've ever seen.

I also wanted a way to be able to simplify information, complement other professionals and create a more cohesive approach to the whole injury problem. Ther wasn't anything available to do what I wanted to achieve, so I created it. I call that approach the "SMARTT® Methods"

 Communication & Coaching Analysis Training – Allows you to develop closer relationships with your clients and see the opportunities for you to contribute to injury prevention within your coaching guidelines

 Movement Development Training – helps you turn ANY exercise or movement into an injury prevention super-move so you can eliminate the need for dedicatin, time to mobility training

 Advanced Movement Analysis & Strength Evolution Training – Creates lightning quick assessments so you can deliver individually targeted and hugely effective advice in seconds – even in a group setting

 Injury Impact & Fallout Training – Taking your coaching skills beyond anything other coaches can dream of and easily build trust & rapport with clients and othe professionals along the way

 Network Building Training – Helping you future-proof your business and become a vital part of any injury management conversation or team

Step #1

The Vault of Injury Prevention Secrets

"Your gateway to a whole new world of opportunity"

Here's a summary of what this training does:

 Gather deeper, more valuable feedback from your clients - You're going to be able to use clues from your clients' body language to decipher potential injury problems long before they become painful

 Discover hidden opportunities – Your existing coaching structure presents so many untapped opportunities. You'll be able to surpass any previous results for your clients and raise the bar for all the other coaches out there!

 Highlight the pitfalls – Too often, coaches are drawn into traps with mobility and injury prevention. You're going to be able to identify them all and easily side-step every single one!

 Elevate potential – Not every coach is prepared for what they'll discover but for those who are ready, you'll be given the chance to shine!

Step #2

SMARTT® Coach Certification

"Transforming the ordinary"

Here's a summary of what this training does:

 Revolutionise Warming Up – This is by far the most overlooked and under utilised area of fitness coaching. You'll be shown how to transform yours so that your clients are more capable of the upcoming workout and preventing injury in half the time

 Eliminate Stretching – You'll discover how to keep your clients safe from injury, without the need for stretching or dedicated mobility training

 Revamp your clients' performances – Use simple tweaks to your existing coaching practices to help your clients get faster and stronger with less effort

 Develop more income streams – Maximise your new skills to expand your sources of income – even if coaching is just a hobby!

Step #3

SMARTT® Coach Technique & Performance Specialist Certification

"Laser Targeted, Lightning Quick"

Here's a summary of what this training does:

 Shatter Illusions About Technique Problems – You'll discover the 3 fundamental factors that underpin ALL the problems you see and develop the skills to deal with them, fast.

 Fortify Strength Training Principles – Evolve your strength training to bullet-proof your clients' movement even under extreme load

 Accelerate Assessments – Make effective assessments of your clients' movements in seconds – even online, to avoid disruption to your clients' training

 Enhance Skill Acquisition – Fast-track the effectiveness of your clients' movement, without the need for endlessly repetitive drills

 Exceed Your Clients' Expectations – No training has ever made your coaching more efficient, targeted and individualised

85

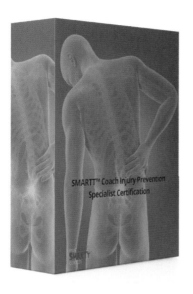

Step #4

SMARTT® Coach Injury Prevention Specialist Certification

"Be the Missing Link"

Here's a summary of what this training does:

 Make it easy for other professionals to work alongside you – Discover what makes them tick, the results they're looking for and how you can easily help them achieve that

 Establish yourself as a leader in your niche – Quickly become the "go-to" coach in your specific area of sport or fitness when it comes to injuries

 Ease your clients' worries – Never before has it been easier to ease your clients' fears around their injury issues so they can get results faster than ever before

 Play a big part in your clients' injury recovery – Take a leading role in shortening injury recovery times for your clients

Step #5

The SMARTT® Communication Mastermind
"The Solution for Your Fitness Business or Club"

Here's a summary of what this training does:

 Create an Unstoppable Stream of Your Dream Clients – Building a network of like-minded professionals, clubs and other coaches will ensure your dream customers find you and are eager to work with you

 Make You an Indispensable Part of the Team – Your results will demonstrate your expertise so that other professionals see you as a vital part of their injury management team

 Focus on the job you love – Creating your own unique ecosystem will ensure that you are positioned within it at your favourite point so you can concentrate on doing the things that you love best

 Brainstorm with others – Surrounding yourself with a small group of other professionals who are trying to achieve the same as you gives you insights and short-cuts you won't find anywhere else

Bonus Step

The SMARTT® Safe Mark

"Instant Recognition"

Here's a summary of what this step does:

 Become the most popular club or fitness business in town: Use the SMARTT® Safe Mark logo to demonstrate your commitment to, and achievement with injury prevention within your club or business which will attract new members/clients

 Get recognised within your sport or fitness niche: Achieving the SMARTT® Safe Mark will demonstrate that your club or business is willing to go above and beyond for their members, which will help you achieve other accolades within the industry

 Be the leader in your niche: When other clubs and businesses see that you have achieved this mark of excellence, they will want that too, which raises everyone's standards

 Establish your reputation of excellence: Build instant trust with brand new clients and other professionals who want to work with you

Amazing!

What's My Next Step?

If You're Ready to Elevate Your Potential and Discover the Hidden Opportunities Within Your Coaching...

Step #1 - Join the Group

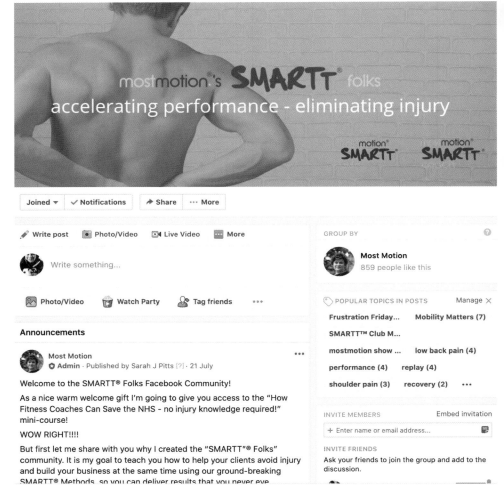

Join us at smarttfolks.com!

If You're Ready to Elevate Your Potential and Discover the Hidden Opportunities Within Your Coaching...

Step #2 - Answer a few simple questions

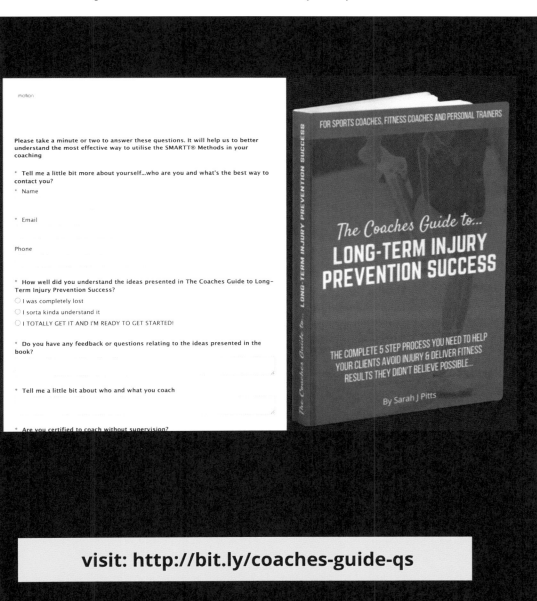

motion

Please take a minute or two to answer these questions. It will help us to better understand the most effective way to utilise the SMARTT® Methods in your coaching

* Tell me a little bit more about yourself...who are you and what's the best way to contact you?
* Name

* Email

Phone

* How well did you understand the ideas presented in The Coaches Guide to Long-Term Injury Prevention Success?
○ I was completely lost
○ I sorta kinda understand it
○ I TOTALLY GET IT AND I'M READY TO GET STARTED!

* Do you have any feedback or questions relating to the ideas presented in the book?

* Tell me a little bit about who and what you coach

* Are you certified to coach without supervision?

FOR SPORTS COACHES, FITNESS COACHES AND PERSONAL TRAINERS

The Coaches Guide to...
LONG-TERM INJURY PREVENTION SUCCESS

THE COMPLETE 5 STEP PROCESS YOU NEED TO HELP YOUR CLIENTS AVOID INJURY & DELIVER FITNESS RESULTS THEY DIDN'T BELIEVE POSSIBLE...

By Sarah J Pitts

visit: http://bit.ly/coaches-guide-qs

With Super Fast Results!

Justine's experience is just one of many that I've had the pleasure of creating over the last few years. She was diagnosed with a painful labral tear in her hip and was struggling to move without significant discomfort.

She had been to see her local therapist, Martin, who was keen for her to avoid surgery and suggested a collagen injection to promote healing within the damaged tissue. The thought of an injection made her nervous and she was desperate to do anything she could to ease the pain.

She'd seen Martin the day before and he'd recommended that she come back in two weeks for the injection, but this left Justine feeling frustrated and alone as she faced the prospect of two whole weeks without pain relief or any kind of action plan...but this is where the SMARTT® Methods shine!

One of the worst feelings for people in pain is one of helplessness and a lack of control - and if we add to that a complete lack of understanding of the condition, the result is that our clients scour the internet for information about what they have and what they should do. But in most cases, this doesn't actually help, in fact, it just leaves our clients feeling more confused than ever and sometimes simply terrified that they have some kind of incurable problem!

This is exactly what happened to Justine.

So, when she asked for my help, the very first thing I did was explain to her WHY the tear had happened in the first place and what Martin was trying to achieve with his collagen injection.

When she felt confident that she understood what was happening in her body I gave her a series of simple movement videos to follow that she could do every day, whenever suited her...as long as all her movement was pain-free.

All the movements were designed to help **relieve the strain on the labrum** and increase blood flow to that area **to promote healing**. None of these movements caused increased strain, were painful in the slightest, or tried in any way to deal directly with the painful area.

After about a week, she mentioned that her thigh didn't feel as tight and that the pain had moved from her hip to an ache in her lower back (which meant that she'd **reduced the strain on her labrum** and her back was just tired from being strained too).

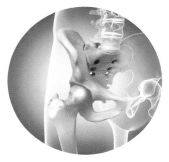

But of course, experiencing this improvement gives rise to hope...and hope leads to more frustrations when you still can't do what you normally would, which leads to more questions!

The problem is, that _most therapists don't have a facility for clients to ask questions_ when they have them, so clients end up having to wait until their next appointment...but fitness coaches have great communication channels with their clients, and that's why Justine felt comfortable pinging me a message about her frustrations.

Within a few hours she had answers to her questions which meant that she was sticking to the programming and confident that she was helping her own situation, rather than worrying that she would hurt herself further (which usually means not doing anything) or doing too much (and hurting herself further) because she didn't understand what was happening.

Just by my being part of the team dealing with this problem, Justine **felt supported and was making progress**. And this in itself made a _massive difference_ to her during this stressful and daunting time in her life - but be under no illusions, in situations like this, movement alone is NOT enough to cure the problem.

But neither was Martin's.

An injection by itself may have helped ease the pain for a little while, but it wouldn't have done anything to remove the major contributing factors to the tear happening in the first place - which means it could easily (and would be very likely to) happen again

And that's why, working together, in **complementary yet completely different capacities** is the BEST way to get the fastest results.

Not all changes can be measured - and that's okay!

Instead of waiting two weeks in agony, with no way of making progress, Justine was able to take immediate and positive action, which **reduced her pain** and put her mind at ease.

Because of that action, at the end of the two weeks her situation could have improved enough for Martin to decide on a different treatment path for the changes in symptoms that she presented. It could have helped the injection be more effective. It could have shortened her recovery by weeks, if not months.

While it's impossible to know the future, we do know this...that **without the SMARTT® Methods, Justine would have spent two weeks worried, in pain and feeling very alone.**

And the craziest thing of all is that **I've never met Martin**, or had any contact with him about this issue, yet I can still support his treatment approach to give Justine the best possible outcome...which is what we ALL want!

Of course, problems like this don't magically disappear overnight, and Justine's situation is ongoing, but we are working together to ensure that this issue, and many others associated with the underlying causes of it, don't happen again.

Revealed!

The True Power of Injury Prevention...

When the ripples of our small actions are felt by everyone...

YOU can help change the world!

The framework I've outlined in this book will help you to build stronger connections with your immediate clients, help them to avoid injury and to establish yourself as a leader in the industry. **But the benefits don't stop there!**

By working together, every fitness coach across the world can be part of a much bigger story that can **have a positive impact on everyone!**

You see, injuries don't just affect our individual clients. They're devastating healthcar systems, businesses and entire economies too - but we have the power to change th

For every individual that we help avoid pain, we're **saving healthcare systems the cost** of appointments, medications, specialists, equipment and all the unseen costs that accumulate as a person's pain gets worse, more prolonged and more debilitatin

We're **saving companies from the loss in productivity and the rising cost of sick days,** which has a direct impact on our economies. And we're **saving generations o older people the devastating blow of losing their independence** as they are force to move out of their own home, into a care facility.

By following this framework, I've been proving for years that **most non-collision injuries are completely avoidable**, yet it's these small aches and pains that seem to appear out of nowhere that are costing our society the most. It's the tight hamstring that develops into a tear, that later develops into knee pain, that eventually develops into osteoarthritis and requires major surgery.

Musculoskeletal injuries like these affect every group of our society. They preve young athletes from following their dreams, they cause working age adults to lose ou financially if they have to miss work, and they strip our elderly population of their independence.

But regardless of the age of the person suffering, **chronic pain increases feelings o anxiety and depression**, which can eventually lead to isolation, loneliness and even addiction to prescription medication.

While everyone else is waiting, we're taking ACTION!

Not to mention the inability to exercise, which cycles them back to the risk of developing all the lifestyle diseases they were trying to avoid in the first place!

As a society, **we've ended up in this mess because we've been waiting for the pain** to come before taking action. But every sports and fitness coach knows that **our clients don't need to be in pain for these problems to affect their ability to exercise**...even the fear of irritating previous pain is enough to destroy motivation and consistency of training.

But waiting for the pain means that **we're missing the opportunity to prevent these problems** - and that's how YOU can help change the world, and show the industry just what can be achieved if we take a more proactive, collaborative approach.

By playing YOUR part and actively trying to prevent these injuries, you'll become part of a collective. And it's **this collective that has the power to change the world**.

Your individual efforts are like throwing a small pebble into a big pond - it'll make small ripples. But **our collective contribution is like hurtling a meteor into the ocean - it'll create a tidal wave!**

It has always been my vision to make sporting injuries across the world the exception rather than the rule, and by everyone working together using the SMARTT® methods we can actually make it happen!

And that means happier, healthier populations who live in societies that don't have to bear the financial and emotional cost of chronic pain. This means that **more money can be spent on schools, hospitals, transport, the environment, opportunities and all the other topics that we care so passionately about.**

So, I guess the question now is, are you ready to join us?

The 5 Steps

So How Did I Do?
Do You Understand the 5 Steps Presented in This Guide?

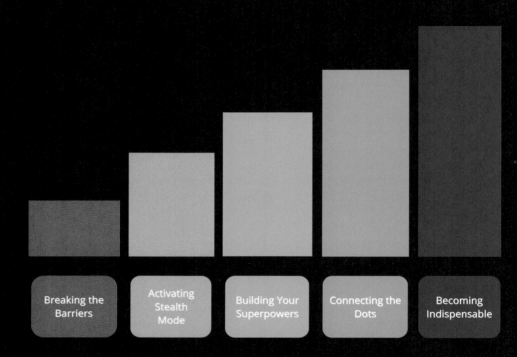

Breaking the Barriers

Activating Stealth Mode

Building Your Superpowers

Connecting the Dots

Becoming Indispensable

You Don't Have to Know How to Put These Steps into Practice, But Do You Understand the Benefits of Each Step?

To Conclude
A Personal Message From Sarah J Pitts

Well, there you go! I hope that you are **BLOWN AWAY** with the potential that has been presented to you in this guide.

If you are, then I highly encourage you to get involved with our community. There is **NO DOUBT** in my mind that this is the solution for you.

If you're feeling overwhelmed...

You might feel like you're drowning in possibilities if you made it this far and that's okay. Remember, **you don't have to understand everything** that was presented in this guide. It took me years to master what was presented here.

The reason I revealed the "5 steps" to you was to get you excited about the possibilities open to you. I wanted you to understand that **I actually have the answer to your problems.**

I've devoted the last 5 years of my life to creating the **trainings, strategies and resources** that I've mentioned in this guide, but you are able to take it as far as you deem necessary.

At least you know you have a roadmap to follow. You know EXACTLY what you can be working towards and you know where to find the solution. For now, I recommend that you join the group and fill in the questionnaire outlined in the previous couple of pages. Make sure you tag me when you say "hi" in the group and let us know what you think of this guide

I want to wish you all the best.

See you in the group!

Are you ready to

GET STARTED?

Start your training at

http://bit.ly/injury-vault-guide

Printed in Great Britain
by Amazon

53383516R00056